ROXIE MUNRO
DESERT DAYS
DESERT NIGHTS

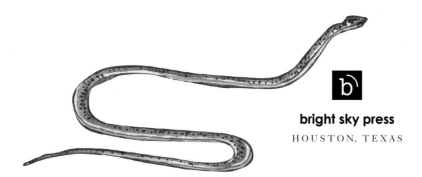

b

bright sky press

HOUSTON, TEXAS

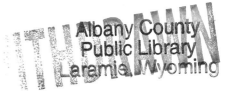

GREAT
BASIN

U.S.A.

DEATH VALLEY

MOJAVE

PAINTED
DESERT

SONORAN

PACIFIC
OCEAN

CHIHUAHUAN

MEXICO

THE DESERTS OF NORTH AMERICA

We often think of a desert as a *hot, arid*, and *uninhabitable* place.

Arid yes. Desert precipitation is, on an average, less than 10 inches a year.

Hot? Yes and no. Deserts often reach scorching temperatures of over a hundred degrees during the day, but can be quite chilly at night. And there are cold deserts—in fact, Antarctica is sometimes considered a desert!

Uninhabitable? Not at all. Though there are few large animals that can withstand the heat or make do with so little water, deserts are full of life—mostly insects, spiders, reptiles, birds, and small burrowing rodents.

Many animals have adapted to the desert: they live without ever drinking water, manage to avoid the sun, and have colors or patterns that help them blend in with the landscape, or reflect, instead of absorb heat.

In this book, we learn about North American deserts. You can see where they are located on the map on the left: the **Sonoran Desert,** the **Mojave** (which includes **Death Valley**), the **Great Basin,** the **Chihuahuan,** and the **Painted Desert.**

At night, the desert becomes a different world. Many creatures are *nocturnal*—they come out after dark, when it cools down. But there are also animals that are *diurnal*—busy during the day.

FIND, NAME, AND COUNT the animals you see during the day, and then find the animals that come out after the sun has set.

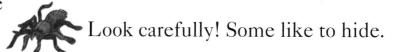 Look carefully! Some like to hide.

ANSWERS are in the back of this book, with fun facts about each desert and the fascinating animals that make these extreme places their home.

CHIHUAHUAN DESERT **DAY**

FIND THESE▶
DAYTIME **CRITTERS**

Desert Spiny Lizard	1 Burrowing Owl	5 Scaled Quail	
2 Horned Toads	1 Harris' Hawk	1 Collared Lizard	1 Yucca Moth
Western Rattlesnake	1 Turkey Vulture	1 Giant Desert Centipede	1 Garter Snake
4 Javelinas	2 Monarch Butterflies	1 Greater Roadrunner	1 Mexican Ground Squirrel

CHIHUAHUAN DESERT NIGHT

FIND THESE
NIGHTTIME CRITTERS

Western Spotted Skunk	1	Western Rattlesnake	1	Black-tailed Jackrabbit	1	Hairy Desert Scorpion
Mexican Free-tailed Bats	1	Desert Banded Gecko	1	Stink Beetle	1	Kit Fox
Porcupine	1	Trapdoor Spider	1	Burrowing Owl	1	Kangaroo Rat	1	Yucca Moth
Desert Cottonails	1	Giant Desert Centipede	1	Coyote	1	Whip Scorpion	3	White-tailed Deer

FIND THESE
DAYTIME **CRITTER**

Rock Wren	1 Kit Fox	3 Western Pygmy	1 Round-tailed Ground Squirrel
Gambel's Quail	1 Scorpion	Blue Butterflies	1 Coachwhip (Red Racer)
Bighorn Sheep	1 Desert Iguana	1 Red-tailed Hawk	1 Zebra-tailed Lizard	1 Side-blotched Lizard
Desert Cottontail	3 Turkey Vultures	1 Chuckwalla	1 Greater Roadrunner	1 Tarantula

GREAT BASIN DESERT **DAY**

Golden Eagle

Collared Lizard

Porcupine

Mormon Cricket

1 Antelope Squirrel

1 Great Basin Wood Nymph

1 Black-billed Magpie

3 Sage Grouse

6 Pronghorn Antelope

1 Bighorn Sheep

1 Yellow-bellied Marmot

1 Pygmy Rabbit

1 Great Basin
   Fritillary Butterfly

1 Coyote

1 Raven

1 Great Basin
   Gopher Snake

GREAT BASIN DESERT NIGHT

MOJAVE DESERT **DAY**

FIND THESE DAYTIME CRITTERS

Ladder-backed		1 Desert Hairy Scorpion	4 Turkey Vultures	1 Chuckwalla	
Woodpecker		7 Harvester Ants	3 Tarantula Hawk Wasps	1 Western Patchnose Snake	
Desert Tortoise		1 Raven	1 Fringe-toed Lizard	1 American Kestrel	2 Mojave Dotted Blue
Antelope Squirrel		1 Coachwhip (Red Racer)	1 Scott's Oriole	1 Long-nosed Leopard Lizard	Butterflies

MOJAVE DESERT NIGHT

FIND THESE NIGHTTIME CRITTERS

Yucca Moth	1	Tarantula	1	Desert Tortoise	1	Bobcat
Desert Hairy Scorpion	1	Coyote	1	Mojave Desert Sidewinder	1	Kangaroo Rat
Black-tailed Jackrabbit	2	Desert Cottontails	1	Desert Woodrat	1	Desert Spider Beetle
California Leaf-nosed Bats	2	Pocket Mice	1	Pocket Gopher	1	Kit Fox

PAINTED DESERT **DAY**

FIND THESE
DAYTIME CRITTERS

Burrowing Owl	1 Western Meadowlark	1 Prairie Falcon	
Bark Scorpion	3 Pipeline Swallowtail	1 Greater Roadrunner	
Collared Lizard	Butterflies	1 Side-blotched	1 Bighorn Sheep
Pronghorn Antelope	1 Striped Skunk	Lizard	1 Plateau Striped Whiptail

FIND THES
NIGHTTIME CRITTER

FIND THES[ ]
DAYTIME CRITTERS[ ]

Antelope Squirrel	1	Elf Owl	4	Turkey Vultures	1	Red-tailed Hawk
Giant Hairy Scorpion	1	Gila Woodpecker	1	Collared Lizard	1	Costa's Hummingbird
Velvet Ants	1	Arizona Coral Snake	5	Gambel's Quail	1	Desert Tortoise	1	Greater Roadrunner
Coati	1	Cactus Wren	1	Sonoran Whipsnake	3	Painted Lady Butterflies	1	Desert Spiny Lizard

CHIHUAHUAN DESERT ANSWERS

The Chihuahuan Desert is the largest and easternmost of all North American deserts. Most of it is in Mexico, but portions extend into Texas, New Mexico and Arizona. Summers in the Chihuahuan Desert are long and hot, but because of its high elevation —half is above 4,000 feet (1,220 meters)—winters can turn freezing cold.

Here, bats abound — voracious eaters like the pallid bat, devouring grasshoppers, scorpions, and large crickets—and in Big Bend in Texas, which is part of the desert, you'll find more species of birds than in any other North American national park.

The landscape is dotted with desert shrubs (bushes like creosote), mesquite trees, and lots of cacti—particularly prickly pear. To keep cool, a prickly pear cactus will angle the direction of its green pads to cut down on exposure to the sun. Another plant, the resurrection plant, curls into a tight brown disc when it's dry. Hours after a rain, stems unroll and it turns green. In the spring, after a rare shower, the desert fills up like a multicolored quilt, with wildflowers.

FUN FACTS

Javelinas (also called collared peccaries or vaquira) can eat cactus with spines because they have tough leather-like skin around their mouths, and their digestive system can pass sharp objects through. They walk single file, one after another, when traveling.

The **Horned Lizard** (or horned toad) can squirt a jet of blood from ducts in the corner of its eye up to three feet away to startle attackers. These small lizards blend in with the background, and are often hard to see.

Termites and **Ants** are particularly abundant in the warm Chihuahuan and Sonoran deserts—they often outnumber all other animals combined.

The **Giant Desert Centipede** can grow to 6 or 8 inches long, but it usually has only about 40 legs, not 100.

When disturbed, the **Stink Beetle** puts its rear end up into the air and a nasty smelly liquid comes out.

Cartoon-looking **Roadrunners** can run up to 15 miles an hour. The long tail acts like a brake, stopping it suddenly, or like a rudder—by flicking it to one side they can turn in mid-stride.

DAY CRITTERS

1. 1 Desert Spiny Lizard
2. 2 Horned Toads
3. 1 Western Rattlesnake
4. 4 Javelinas
5. 1 Burrowing Owl
6. 1 Harris' Hawk
7. 1 Turkey Vulture
8. 2 Monarch Butterflies
9. 5 Scaled Quail
10. 1 Collared Lizard
11. 1 Giant Desert Centipede
12. 1 Greater Roadrunner
13. 1 Yucca Moth
14. 1 Garter Snake
15. 1 Mexican Ground Squirrel

NIGHT CRITTERS

1. 1 Western Spotted Skunk
2. 5 Mexican Free-tailed Bats
3. 1 Porcupine
4. 2 Desert Cottontails
5. 1 Western Rattlesnake
6. 1 Desert Banded Gecko
7. 1 Trapdoor Spider
8. 1 Giant Desert Centipede
9. 1 Black-tailed Jackrabbit
10. 1 Stink Beetle
11. 1 Burrowing Owl
12. 1 Coyote
13. 1 Hairy Desert Scorpion
14. 1 Kit Fox
15. 1 Kangaroo Rat
16. 1 Whip Scorpion
17. 1 Yucca Moth
18. 3 White-tailed Deer

CHIHUAHUAN DESERT **DAY**

CHIHUAHUAN DESERT **NIGHT**

In the northern part of the Mojave Desert you'll find one of the hottest places on earth—with the highest recorded temperature in the Western Hemisphere, and maybe the world: 134 F (56.7 C). Not only is this place really hot, it is extremely dry, with an average rainfall of less than 2 inches. Many early travelers got lost here, and even perished, which is how, in the 1850s, it got its name, Death Valley.

When rain falls in the surrounding mountains, salt washes out and ends up on the valley floor, creating "salt flats." There are also sand dunes, canyons, badlands, rocky ridges, and a few spring-fed wetlands. This is where you'll find the lowest land in North America. It's called Badwater, and lies almost 300 feet below sea level. Despite such extreme conditions, more than 1,000 plant varieties live in Death Valley—many especially adapted for living in salty soil, like pickleweed and saltbush. Some plants have roots that go down 10 times the height of a person to collect water. Some have a root system just below the desert floor that extends out in all directions.

FUN FACTS

The Desert Iguana is darker when it is cold to absorb warm sunlight, and when its body temperature rises, it becomes lighter, to reflect the sun.

The **Red Racer** is also called a coachwhip snake—not poisonous, but it's fast, and it bites!

Scorpions get enough water from eating and digesting their prey; they don't have to drink.

When threatened by a predator, some Desert Geckos can "drop," or amputate, their own tail. But the dropped tail doesn't just lie there—it can make movements (swing back and forth, and flip up in the air) for up to half an hour, to distract the predator.

Turkey Vultures have great eyesight and a keen sense of smell.

Sidewinder Rattlesnakes move fast along hot dunes, propelling themselves head forward, and dragging their body behind to minimize contact with the hot sand and provide traction.

Do you know why any animals in hot deserts (like the **Jackrabbit**, Mule Deer, and **Kit Fox**) have large ears? Because blood circulating in the ears helps keep the animal cool.

Some small creatures, like **Beetles** and Lizards, reduce the amount of heat they absorb from the desert surface by having long legs to keep them high up and to disperse heat. Pale-colored fur and feathers help others to keep cool by reflecting sunlight.

DAY CRITTERS

1. 1 Rock Wren
2. 3 Gambel's Quail
3. 1 Bighorn Sheep
4. 1 Desert Cottontail
5. 1 Kit Fox
6. 1 Scorpion
7. 1 Desert Iguana
8. 3 Turkey Vultures
9. 3 Western Pygmy Blue Butterflies
10. 1 Red-tailed Hawk
11. 1 Chuckwalla
12. 1 Round-tailed Ground Squirrel
13. 1 Coachwhip (Red Racer)
14. 1 Zebra-tailed Lizard
15. 1 Greater Roadrunner
16. 1 Side-blotched Lizard
17. 1 Tarantula

NIGHT CRITTERS

1. 1 Desert Shrew
2. 4 Pallid Bats
3. 1 Bobcat
4. 2 Desert Cottontails
5. 1 Pocket Mouse
6. 1 Scorpion
7. 1 Sidewinder
8. 1 White-lined Sphinx Moth
9. 1 Black-tailed Jackrabbit
10. 2 Desert Banded Geckos
11. 1 Kangaroo Rat
12. 1 Stink Beetle
13. 1 Badger
14. 1 Kit Fox
15. 1 Tarantula
16. 1 Red-spotted Toad
17. 1 Coyote

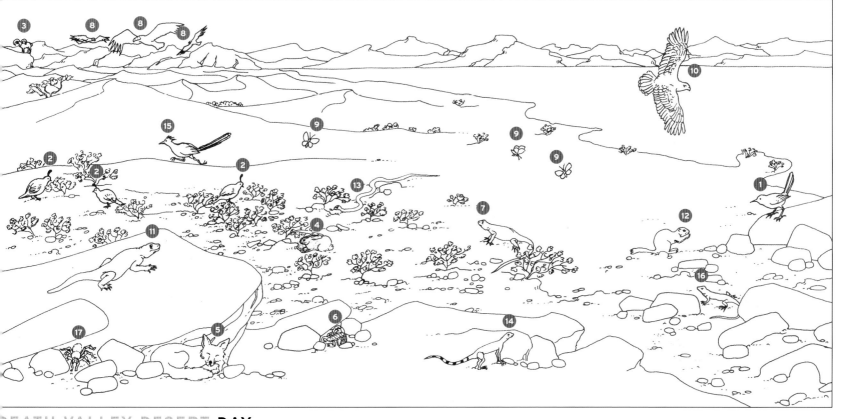

DEATH VALLEY DESERT **DAY**

DEATH VALLEY DESERT **NIGHT**

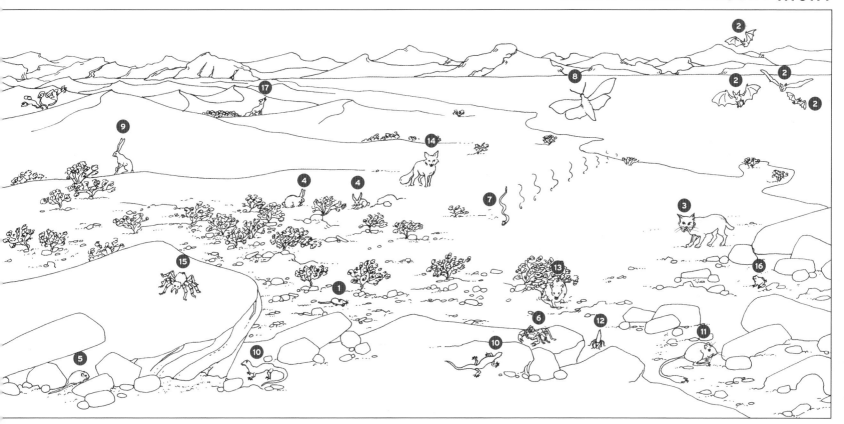

GREAT BASIN DESERT ANSWERS

Don't expect to see many cacti, and don't look for a lot of flowers—just sagebrush, rocks and mountains, and trees like pine, spruce, juniper, and fir. The Great Basin Desert is a large, high, cold desert, with a short growing season in the spring, a dry summer, and a cold winter. Most of the precipitation comes down as snow, not rain.

Spread across valleys and mountains (some over 13,000 feet), the Great Basin is the largest desert in the United States, mainly in Nevada, but also in California, Idaho, Oregon, Utah, and Arizona, occupying approximately 160,000 square miles. It has less variety of animals and plants than any of the other deserts in the Northern Hemisphere, and is one of the most sparsely populated regions of the United States. But because of its remote location, away from the light pollution caused by cities and towns, and its cold clear skies, the Great Basin is one of the best places in America for stargazing.

FUN FACTS

A **Gray Fox** can climb 50 feet up a limbless tree trunk. Then it can jump from limb to limb, like a cat or a squirrel, to escape from predators.

There are a dozen or so species of rattlesnakes in North American deserts. The Western Diamondback is the largest and can grow up to seven feet in length. It rattles with its strong tail muscles when threatened. A new segment in the tail is formed every time the snakes molts.

Some animals, like **Spadefoot Toads**, estivate (sleep) during the hottest, driest months. And in the cold deserts, some animals hibernate, or sleep through the winter, in a protected place.

Snakes don't have ears, but are sensitive to ground vibrations, so they can feel danger, or even the approach of dinner!

Bats are the only mammals that can truly fly. To "see" at night they use a form of sonar —they send out a sound and listen for it to bounce off objects. They like to sleep hanging upside down, and although most live about ten years, some species can live to be 30.

The Woodrat is called a pack rat because it collects all kinds of items for its nest, like bones, sticks, dung, leaves, and other small objects found in deserts—even coins, keys, or jewelry, if you drop them!

Bighorn Sheep are known for head-to-head combat between males, which can last for more than 24 hours. A ram's horns grow longer every year; they can weigh up to 30 pounds, as much as the rest of the body bones combined. They have two toes on each foot, which can spread wide for support and have rough pads so they can grip the ground and travel around on uneven rocky terrain.

DAY CRITTERS

1. 1 Golden Eagle
2. 1 Collared Lizard
3. 1 Porcupine
4. 1 Mormon Cricket
5. 1 Antelope Squirrel
6. 1 Great Basin Wood Nymph
7. 1 Black-billed Magpie
8. 3 Sage Grouse
9. 6 Pronghorn Antelope
10. 1 Bighorn Sheep
11. 1 Yellow-bellied Marmot
12. 1 Pygmy Rabbit
13. 1 Great Basin Fritillary Butterfly
14. 1 Coyote
15. 1 Raven
16. 1 Great Basin Gopher Snake

NIGHT CRITTERS

1. 1 Tarantula
2. 1 Desert Woodrat
3. 4 Townsend's Big-eared Bat
4. 1 Western Rattlesnake
5. 1 Great Basin Spadefoot Toad
6. 1 Gray Fox
7. 5 Mule Deer
8. 1 Black-tailed Jackrabbit
9. 3 Desert Cottontails
10. 1 Coyote
11. 1 Mountain Lion
12. 1 Kangaroo Rat
13. 2 Pocket Mice

GREAT BASIN DESERT **DAY**

GREAT BASIN DESERT **NIGHT**

MOJAVE DESERT ANSWERS

The Mojave Desert, named after the Native American Mojave tribe, is the highest, driest and smallest of the main four North American deserts. It is found in various parts of California, Nevada, Utah, and Arizona, and is called a "High Desert" because of its high altitude—averaging 3,000 feet (9000 meters) to 5,500 feet (1,700 meters).

There are a variety of habitats here, from mesas, to salt flats, and sand dunes. The surrounding mountains block most rain—one California town, now deserted, once went almost two years without a drop of rain. There are several ghost towns in the Mojave desert—besides little rain, hot long summers and cold winters, the desert, particularly the western part, can have winds above 50 mph, so it can be inhospitable to live in.

Because it gets cold in the winter, with some snow, there are lots of bushes, but few cacti. Almost a quarter of plants in the Mojave Desert are unique to it. They are found nowhere else in the world. The most famous is the Joshua tree—the tall spiny yucca you see in these paintings.

FUN FACTS

The **Fringe-toed Lizard** can dash over sand up to 15 mph. To keep sand out, it has special nasal valves that can close, earflaps, protective eyelids and a recessed jaw. It dives down into the loose sand in the dunes and "swims" down to cooler depths, and can stay buried for a long time—breathing air trapped in the tiny spaces between the grains of sand.

When threatened, the **Chuckwalla** sneaks into crevices between rocks, inflates its body by gulping air, and stays wedged in the small space so tightly it can't be pulled out by a predator.

There are **Cockroaches** in the desert—they live underground in the sandy soil, where it is cool, and they can absorb water through the damp sand.

To protect itself from strong sun, the **White-tailed Antelope Squirrel** shades itself with its bushy tail.

In very hot weather, some creatures, like the **Western Tortoise** and **Vultures**, urinate on their legs—the evaporation cools them off.

Harvester Ants dig maze-like tunnel systems in the soil, sometimes as deep as 15 feet down. They store the seeds they collect in grain rooms. There are other rooms like nurseries to develop larve and nurture eggs.

DAY CRITTERS

1. 1 Ladder-backed Woodpecker
2. 1 Desert Tortoise
3. 1 Antelope Squirrel
4. 1 Desert Hairy Scorpion
5. 7 Harvester Ants
6. 1 Raven
7. 2 Mojave Dotted Blue Butterflies
8. 1 Coachwhip (Red Racer)
9. 4 Turkey Vultures
10. 3 Tarantula Hawk Wasps
11. 1 Fringe-toed Lizard
12. 1 Scott's Oriole
13. 1 Chuckwalla
14. 1 Western Patchnose Snake
15. 1 American Kestrel
16. 1 Long-nosed Leopard Lizard

NIGHT CRITTERS

1. 1 Yucca Moth
2. 1 Desert Hairy Scorpion
3. 1 Black-tailed Jackrabbit
4. 2 California Leaf-nosed Bats
5. 1 Tarantula
6. 1 Coyote
7. 2 Desert Cottontails
8. 2 Pocket Mice
9. 1 Desert Tortoise
10. 1 Mojave Desert Sidewinder
11. 1 Desert Woodrat
12. 1 Pocket Gopher
13. 1 Bobcat
14. 1 Kangaroo Rat
15. 1 Desert Spider Beetle
16. 1 Kit Fox

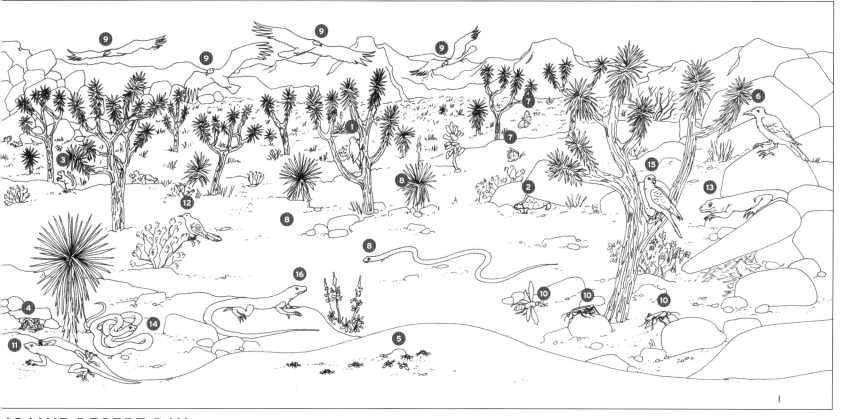

MOJAVE DESERT DAY

MOJAVE DESERT NIGHT

PAINTED DESERT ANSWERS

Beginning near the Grand Canyon, the Painted Desert is a wind- and water-sculpted expanse of badland hills, flat-topped mesas, and buttes. It stretches southeast in Arizona for over 160 miles, and includes parts of the Petrified Forest. Barren and austere, the Painted Desert is actually considered a grassland ecosystem, rather than a desert, but it's very arid, and has little vegetation.

It's easy to see how the Painted Desert got its name. Color is everywhere—layer upon layer of vibrant hues of yellow, red, pink, blue, and lavender. Sometimes described as "multi-colored layer cakes," these patterns are due to minerals in the rocks—for example, limonite creates yellow, hematite gives you red, and gypsum makes white stripes. There's also a blue section of the desert. The best time to see this spectacular show of colors, created by nature over millions and millions of years, is late afternoon or early evening, when, if you are standing on a bluff or hiking, the whole world becomes magical.

FUN FACTS

Scorpions and **Large Spiders** have "book lungs." Folds in the abdomen, like pages in a book, provide surface for gas exchange to the tissues and are helpful in preventing water loss.

The **Pronghorn Antelope** is one of the fastest animals in North America—like a car, it can sprint up to 60 mph!

There are more **Lizards** in North American deserts than any other animal.

The largest desert spider is the **Fuzzy Tarantula**. Its leg span can be six inches across—bigger than your hand. There are about 20 different kinds of tarantulas in the Southwest US. They can live to be 30 years old.

Tiny **Kangaroo Rats** never need to drink water. They get moisture from the insects, plants, and seeds they eat. Specialized kidneys allow the disposal of waste with very little loss of water. They are often seen crossing roads at night, balancing with their furry tails as they hop on strong elongated hind legs. A kangaroo rat can jump up to 10 feet in a single bound, and can swing its rudder-like tail and rapidly change direction.

Coyotes howl at night to let other coyotes know where they are. They travel a long way to hunt and have great eyesight, a keen sense of smell, and excellent hearing. They are found in all of the deserts in this book.

DAY CRITTERS

1. 1 Burrowing Owl
2. 1 Bark Scorpion
3. 1 Collared Lizard
4. 3 Pronghorn Antelope
5. 1 Western Meadowlark
6. 3 Pipeline Swallowtail Butterflies
7. 1 Striped Skunk
8. 1 Prairie Falcon
9. 1 Greater Roadrunner
10. 1 Side-blotched Lizard
11. 1 Bighorn Sheep
12. 1 Plateau Striped Whiptail

NIGHT CRITTERS

1. 1 Giant Desert Centipede
2. 1 Kangaroo Rat
3. 10 Pallid Bats
4. 1 Coyote
5. 1 Black-tailed Jackrabbit
6. 1 Tarantula
7. 1 Bark Scorpion
8. 1 Great Horned Owl
9. 3 Canyon Mice
10. 1 Desert Shrew
11. 1 Bushy-tailed Woodrat
12. 1 Painted Desert Glossy Snake
13. 1 Bobcat

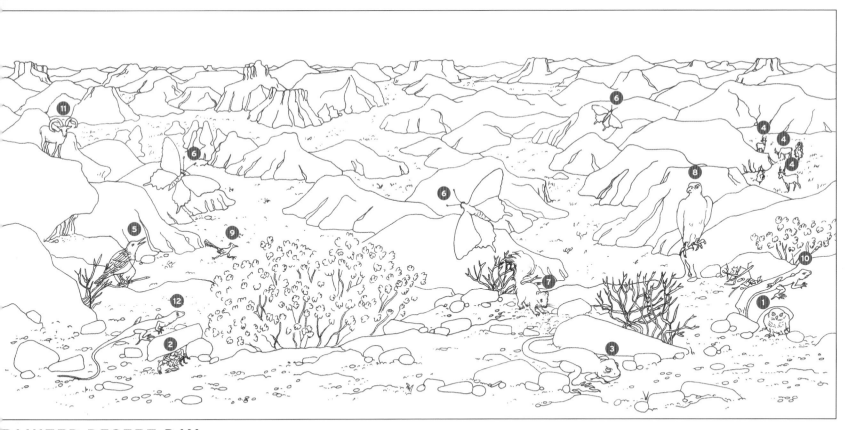

PAINTED DESERT **DAY**

PAINTED DESERT **NIGHT**

SONORAN DESERT ANSWERS

The Sonoran Desert stretches through California, Arizona, and continues into Mexico. It is really hot! In the summer the temperature can reach a sizzling 120 F (49 C), and during the winter it rarely gets below freezing.

No other desert on earth has such a variety of plants. The giant saguaro cactus grows slowly—only six inches in ten years!—but can reach 50 feet (15 meters) tall, and can live over 200 years. Other cacti found here include the pipe organ cactus, with flowers that open at night and are visited by bats, and the spiniest of them all, the teddy bear cholla. The ocotillo (which, after a rainfall, sprouts red flowers at the tops of its tall skinny stems), yuccas (pointy leaves that hurt if you get stuck!), and fishhook barrel cacti that lean toward the sun are other unusual plants.

The Sonoran Desert is home to 130 species of mammals, 20 amphibians, and 100 or more kinds of reptiles. It's one of the richest areas for birds—over 500 kinds—including many hummingbirds.

FUN FACTS

Gila Woodpeckers make holes in saguaro trunks. Each year, after they raise their young, they abandon their home and other animals, like elf owls, bats, lizards, packrats, and mice move in.

The **Arizona Coral Snake** has the strongest venom of any US desert snake, but this elusive snake is seldom seen.

A **Ringtale** isn't a cat—it's a member of the raccoon family. A good climber, it can turn its hind feet backward, and, using sharp claws to grasp on to the bark, go headfirst down a tree trunk.

The **Cactus Wren** builds a football-sized nest (made of grass stems and lined with feathers) in the crook of a saguaro arm or a spiny cholla cactus. They don't get hurt by cactus spines because they have bony feet and a thick coat of feathers.

The **Elf Owl** is the smallest owl in the world—only 5" high, it could fit in the palm of your hand. It lives in old woodpecker holes in saguaro cacti, and eats centipedes, insects and even scorpions. Before feeding a baby owl a scorpion, the mom rips the stinger off.

The **Gila Monster** is the largest and the only poisonous lizard in the US. The poison comes through grooves in its teeth—it bites down and grinds its jaws to kill prey. It eats as much as possible, and stores extra food in its fat tail.

DAY CRITTERS

1. 1 Antelope Squirrel
2. 1 Giant Hairy Scorpion
3. 5 Velvet Ants
4. 3 Coati
5. 1 Elf Owl
6. 1 Gila Woodpecker
7. 1 Arizona Coral Snake
8. 1 Cactus Wren
9. 4 Turkey Vultures
10. 1 Collared Lizard
11. 5 Gambel's Quail
12. 1 Sonoran Whipsnake
13. 1 Red-tailed Hawk
14. 1 Costa's Hummingbird
15. 1 Desert Tortoise
16. 3 Painted Lady Butterflies
17. 1 Greater Roadrunner
18. 1 Desert Spiny Lizard

NIGHT CRITTERS

1. 1 Gila Monster
2. 1 Tarantula
3. 1 Elf Owl
4. 2 Spotted Bats
5. 1 Ringtail
6. 2 Desert Cottontails
7. 1 Desert Tortoise
8. 1 Great Horned Owl
9. 1 Coyote
10. 1 White-lined Sphinx Moth
11. 1 Desert Banded Gecko
12. 1 Arizona Coral Snake
13. 1 Giant Hairy Scorpion
14. 1 Sonoran Green Toad
15. 1 Stink Beetle
16. 1 Bailey's Pocket Mouse
17. 1 Desert Shrew

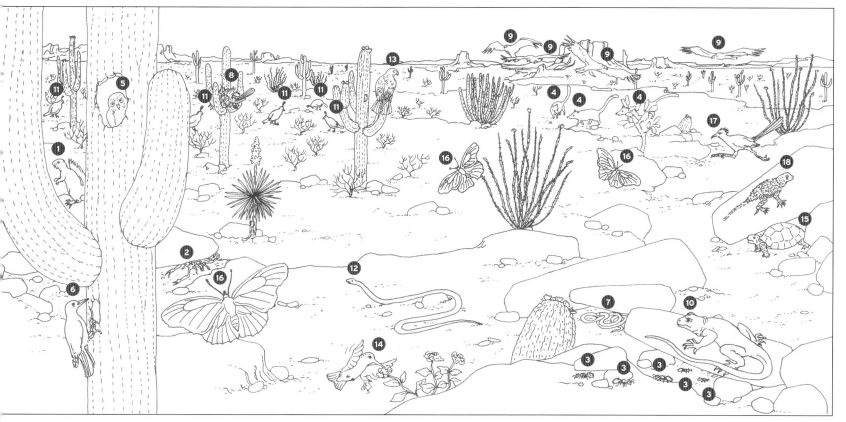

SONORAN DESERT **DAY**

SONORAN DESERT **NIGHT**

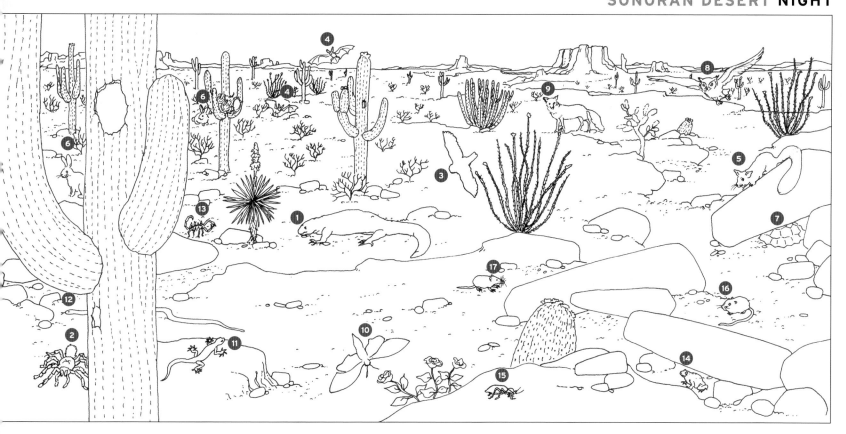

HELPFUL BOOKS AND WEBSITES

Start with these sources to learn more about North American deserts:

BOOKS

Jablonsky, Alice. *101 Questions About Desert Life*, Western National Parks Association, 1994.

Laybach, Christyna & Rene; Smith, Charles W. G. *Raptor!* Storey Publishing, 2002.

Macquity, Miranda. *Desert*, Eyewitness Books, Dorling Kindersley, 1994.

Peterson, Roger Tory. *A Field Guide to the Birds of Texas and Adjacent States*, Houghton Mifflin, 1988.

Wallace, Marianne D. *America's Deserts: Guide to Plants and Animals*, Fulcrum Kids, 1996.

Sowell, John. *Desert Ecology*, The University of Utah Press, 2001.

WEBSITES

National Park Service nps.gov

World Wildlife Fund worldwildlife.org

All Deserts desertusa.com

Sonoran Desert desertmuseum.org
    americansouthwest.net/arizona/sonoran_desert/national_monument.html

Chihuahuan Desert dcdri.org/Desert
    big.bend.national-park.com texasstateparks.gov/big_bend_ranch/

Mojave Desert and Death Valley digital-desert.com
    death.valley.national-park.com/ npca.org/parks/mojave-national-preserve.html

Painted Desert petrified.forest.national-park.com

Great Basin great.basin.national-park.com/bird.htm#mamm
    great.basin.national-park.com/